Poetry
for the
Thoughtful Young

Sit with me, come and see,
It is time for a story.
Take my hand, come and look,
It is time for a book.
Sit with me, come and see,
Snuggled close together.
Take my hand, come and look.
Let us share this good book!

Storytime Song
by Sheila Kerwin
Sung to the tune of Brahms' "Lullaby"

Also from B Cubed Press

Alternative Truths
More Alternative Truths: Tales From the
Resistance
After the Orange: Ruin and Recovery
Alternative Theology
Digging Up My Bones,
by Gwyndyn T. Alexander
Firedancer,
by S.A. Bolich
Alternative Apocalypses
Stories for the Thoughtful Young

Poetry
for the
Thoughtful Young

Edited by
Diana Payton and Bob Brown

Special Thanks
to
Rebecca McFarland Kyle

Cover Design
Bob Brown

Published by

B Cubed Press
Kiona, WA

To my Brahms

Who listened to me read (and occasionally sing) all the poems we considered for this volume. May they bring years of joy.

Diana Payton

Poetry for the Thoughtful Young

Copyright

Publisher's Introduction

As a child, I read.

I loved not only stories, but epic poems and as I grew older I discovered even more. Who can ever forget Shel Silverstein's "Sister for Sale." Having had eight of them, it seemed to be fitting at the time.

Living in a world where the television got two channels, barely, and the only screens in the house were on doors and windows, I loved the heavy dark books I found in a box in the basement.

My favorite was a thick green volume called *Prose and Poetry.* I read it through more times than I have memory of.

It was a book of stories and poems meant for another generation but I loved the words, the glossy pages, the detailed images.

Like all young readers I found reading to be a transport in time and space. A chance to stand beside Horatio on the Bridge and stride forth from Troy with Hector.

Time dims the memories of the detail, but not the pleasure of those worlds.

In this volume Diana Payton and I have the opportunity to give memories to a new generation. The poetry in this volume brings back the joy of reading Shel Silverstein, Robert Frost and other writers of our youth.

But it wasn't just Bob and Diana, Becky Kyle pitched in and was of great assistance in pulling the book together. A special thanks.

So enough, it is time to read, to experience what Diana and I already have: the joy of reading these poems for the first time and then sharing them with others, whether with your grandchild under a quilt, or gift to someone you know will find the time to visit these other worlds that these wonderful writers have conjured for us all.

Poetry for the Thoughtful Young

Table of Contents

A Playground Awaits 1
Melanie Harding-Shaw

I Want to Pat a Polar Bear 3
Robert Dawson

This is the World of Midgard 5
Jim Johnston

Kelpies Crossing 9
Jane Yolen

The Mayor of the Moon 11
Maggie Maxwell

I Like Me 13
Delaren Siverson

I Want to Be a Witch 17
Yuvia Hernández Cháirez
(Translated by Toshiya Kamei)

Dance with the Dinosaurs 19
Isobel Horsburgh

Nigel Neath 21
Paul A. Freeman

Origami Rockets 23
Bruce Boston

Song of the Wall 25
Varya Kartishai

My Most Favorite Thing in the Whole Wide World 27
Elena Sichrovsky

Poetry for the Thoughtful Young

Paper, Ink, and Time 29
Mary Da Prato

Conrad the Dachshund Steps Out 31
Nancy Brewka-Clark

Slaying Dragons (What She Thought) 33
Nancy Binzen

Life is Perpetual Motion 35
Steve Denehan

What Would You Do with a Mini Canoe? 37
Rob Carney

The Duties of a Cat 39
Jenny Blackford

The Toddler's Lament 41
Emily Martha Sorensen

Heavy Weather 43
Bruce Boston

Fairy Tale 45
Gwyndyn Alexander

Do 49
McCollonough Ceili

Nursery Rhyme 51
Shefali Poojary

The Color of My Skin 53
Rucha Dixit

The Kraken 55
Emily Martha Sorensen

Upstarts 57
Jane Yolen

Poetry for the Thoughtful Young

God, the Girl, and the Pony 59
Margaret Cook and Annette Ilowiecki

The Parrot 61
Heather Wastie

Diamonds and Toads: The Sequel 63
Lorraine Schein

Innocent Choice: for Kate Emily Yuan 65
yuan changming

Moon Snail Charioteer 67
Meggie Nelson

A Mouse in Granny's House 69
Sylvia Rouss

Peekaboo Monster 73
Lorna Wood

Grinner King Rictus 75
Daniel Hale

Twenty-Four-Hour Taco Stand 77
Evan Baughfman

Robber Girl 79
Jane Yolen

A Dragon at the Gate 81
Gregg Chamberlain

I Should be King 85
Elinor Clark

The Collective Memories of Reptile-Kind 89
M.X. Kelly

Poetry for the Thoughtful Young

Tale of the Town of Brigsby 91
Stephanie L. Weippert

Tea 95
Steve Denehan

My Dinosaur Day 97
Katey Thompson

Air Conditioning 101
Elizabeth Glann

The Droplet 103
Wenlin Tan

Goodnight, Grandmother Moon 107
Maighread MacKay

The End? 109
Nancy Binzen

A Playground Awaits

By Melanie Harding-Shaw

A swing sways in the gentle breeze in

an empty playground longing for its children.

Ant-like, you will swarm its structures, hanging
from them as if an

anti-gravity ray holds you suspended above the lava
ground. Your

antics will sate its longing until you abandon it once
more. A playground is perpetual

anticipation.

I Want to Pat a Polar Bear

By Robert Dawson

I want to pat a polar bear,
I want to hug a whale,
I want a baby turtle who
Will swim inside my pail.

> *But whales are much too big, my dear,*
> *And polar bears can bite,*
> *And if the turtle missed its mom*
> *It wouldn't sleep at night.*

I want to go to Venus,
I want to go to Mars,
I want to go to Jupiter
And out among the stars.

> *But Venus is too hot, my dear,*
> *And Mars is very cold,*
> *And if we get to Jupiter*
> *It won't be 'til you're old.*

I want to keep the forest green,
And let the stream flow free.
I want to help the weather stay
The way it ought to be.

You only have two hands, my dear,
And that's a lot to do.
But if we work together, we
Can help it all come true.

We'll try to leave the trees to grow,
And guard the little stream.
We'll walk, or bike, or take the bus,
And use less gasoline.

We'll buy things we can use again
And throw less junk away,
And maybe then tomorrow will
Be better than today.

This is the World of Midgard

By Jim Johnston

This is the ice
That lies in the world of Midgard.

This is the cow
That licked the ice
That lies in the world of Midgard.

This the jotun[1]
That sucked at the cow
That licked the ice
That lies in the world of Midgard.

These are the gods[2]
That slew the jotun
That sucked at the cow
That licked the ice
That lies in the world of Midgard.

These are the trees of the human race
Transformed by the gods
That slew the jotun
That sucked at the cow
That licked the ice
That lies in the world of Midgard.

Sun and Moon that shine with grace
Upon the trees of the human race
Transformed by the gods
That slew the jotun
That sucked at the cow
That licked the ice
That lies in the world of Midgard.

Skoll and Hati, the wolves, give chase
To Sun and Moon that shine with grace
Upon the trees of the human race
Transformed by the gods
That slew the jotun
That sucked at the cow
That licked the ice
That lies in the world of Midgard.

The dwarves have delved 'neath the
mountain's face,
Skoll and Hati, the wolves, give chase
To Sun and Moon that shine with grace
Upon the trees of the human race
Transformed by the gods
That slew the jotun
That sucked at the cow
That licked the ice
That lies in the world of Midgard.

The Rainbow Bridge joins place to place,
The dwarves have delved 'neath the
mountain's face,
Skoll and Hati, the wolves, give chase
To Sun and Moon that shine with grace
Upon the trees of the human race
Transformed by the gods
That slew the jotun

That sucked at the cow
That licked the ice
That lies in the world of Midgard.

Yggdrasill soars from leaf to base,
The Rainbow Bridge joins place to place,
The dwarves have delved 'neath the
mountain's face,
Skoll and Hati, the wolves, give chase
To Sun and Moon that shine with grace
Upon the trees of the human race
Transformed by the gods
That slew the jotun
That sucked at the cow
That licked the ice
That lies in the world of Midgard.

1   Jotun is the Norse name for a giant
2   That is, the sons of Bor.

Poetry for the Thoughtful Young

Kelpies Crossing

By Jane Yolen

The sign stood
between loch
and road,
a bit beaten about,
as if gnawed.
The generous letters,
in gothic script,
invoked a Celtic past.
I waited behind a beech
as mist rose over the water.
Remembered my scientist husband
saying that if he could believe
in faeries, this was the place.
And me warning him
against climbing on the back
of any horse rising up
from the dark waters.
Neither of us trusted
the myths, tried to read
cultural shifts in the tales.
But now I hear soft footfalls
of an unshod animal.
If it wants to take me
down to the depths,
I am ready to ride.

Poetry for the Thoughtful Young

The Mayor of the Moon

By Maggie Maxwell

The mayor of the moon
Had his breakfast at noon
With bacon, an egg, and some toast.

The bacon asked
For steak in a glass
And a basket of cranberry roast.

The toast's big demand
Was a sprinkle of sand
On a salad of banana wine.

The egg had a plate
With dried flour and a date
And claimed that his meal was quite fine.

Then the bacon threw fits
Said this meal was the pits
And demanded a new breakfast hour.

"A breakfast at nine,"
Said the toast, "would be fine"
While the egg just picked at its flour.

The mayor of the moon
Held elections in June
'Gainst the bacon, the toast, and the egg.

The bacon was loved.
The egg pushed and shoved
To be noticed around the toast.

But the toast told bad jokes,
The egg had no yolks,
And the bacon was not a good host.

They counted the votes
From the hen and the goats
Good citizens of the moon.

The mayor won again,
Shook hands with the hen
And still dined on his breakfast at noon.

I Like Me

By Delaren Siverson

I like me.
I like my smile.
I like my hair.
I like my arms, my legs, my dimples.
But mostly, I like my heart.
I'm a good person.
I care. I love. I laugh. I cry.

So when Jason called me fat,
It hurt.
When he said, "Put down that donut and
eat a carrot,"
It hurt.
When he said nobody will ever marry me.
It hurt.
But then Meaghan stood up.
She's the prettiest girl at our school.
She told him to be quiet.
I smiled...a little.

She told him I was beautiful.
I smiled a little more.
She told him I was sweet.
She told him I was nice.
She said I was the best friend anyone
could have.
She smiled at me.
She said someday I would make a
beautiful bride.

Then she took my hand, and together we
went outside to play.

The next day, I wore my favorite dress.
It was blue with white trim and lots of
pretty colors,
And when I twirled, it fanned out like a
rainbow covering the sky.
But Jason started laughing.
He said I looked like I was wearing a big,
ugly tent.
He called me a whale.
Meaghan got real mad.
She balled her fists. I thought steam was
gonna shoot out of her ears.

But before she could say a word, Alex
stood up.
Alex is Jason's best friend.
He said that was a very mean thing to say.
He told him to remember when he first got
his glasses
and all the mean things people said to
him.

Jason frowned.
He asked him to remember how much it
hurt.
And how bad it made him feel.
He told Jason he was being a bully.
And he didn't want a bully for a friend

Jason dropped his head.
He sighed.
He told me he was sorry.
Then he turned and walked away.
But I heard him say, "Blue is my favorite
color."

I smiled.

Poetry for the Thoughtful Young

I Want to Be a Witch

by Yuvia Hernández Cháirez (Translated by Toshiya Kamei)

Mom, I want to be a witch
in a fairy tale
who knows witchery, astronomy,
and other tricks.
She can fly to the moon
like an astronaut
or a bird in the sky.
A witch who can
see what happens on the other side,
and trace colors
in the starry sky.

Mom, I want to be a witch,
ugly and old, but brainy
enough to stay clear
of the trap of life.
I want to be someone
everyone looks up to,
someone who can touch the sea
without letting it go.

Mom, I don't want to be a princess
in a fairy tale
who has to wait for her prince
to make all her dreams come true
and doesn't try to live beyond
the daily grind of housework
with kids clinging to her skirt,
obedient with no thought for tomorrow.

Don't give me that look!
I don't want to be a princess,
because I want to be a witch!
Because I want to fly to the moon
on my own wings.

Mom, I don't want to be a princess.
I want to be a witch
in a fairy tale.
I want to be free to fly through the
heavens
like her.

Dance with the Dinosaurs

By Isobel Horsburgh

Dance with the dinosaurs,
Bare your teeth and spread your claws.
Dance like the dinosaurs,
Shake the forest floor.

Dance like a pterodactyl,
Flap your wings and snap your bill.
Swoop like a pterodactyl,
Over the forest floor.

Dance like the iguanadon,
Stomp that foot with the big toes on.
Clomp like the iguanadon,
Pound the forest floor.

Dance like a stegosaur,
Swish your tail and give a roar.
Romp like a stegosaur,
Shake the forest floor.

Dance with the dinosaurs,
Brontosaurus join the chorus.
Dance with the dinosaurs,
Shake the forest floor.

Poetry for the Thoughtful Young

Nigel Neath

By Paul A. Freeman

Nigel Neath lost all his teeth
through eating too much candy;
he threw his toothbrush in the bin
and thought it rather dandy.

But now he cannot chew his food
or else his gums get tender,
so everything he wants to eat
his mum puts in the blender.

Poetry for the Thoughtful Young

Origami Rockets

By Bruce Boston

They float to the moon
in origami rockets.
Astronauts from

a childhood fantasy.
The moon smells
like a green apple.

They walk freely
on its skin without
helmets or spacesuits.

They build a town.
Stores and houses.
Schools and libraries.

A street fair with
lots of free parking.
And the moon people

come to live there.
Up from their craters
and their moon caves.

A gentle sleepy race.
Just the right sort
to carry our dreams.

Poetry for the Thoughtful Young

Song of the Wall

by Varya Kartishai

When I was two,
I was very, very new.
Mama smiled through the crib bars at me.
Those bars were made of wood.
They were training bars, and good.
Now at five, I'm a refugee.

We trudged down the road.
Seeking work in any mode,
So that we could breathe free.
But the guards took me away,
Though my mama wept and prayed.
Now at five, I'm a refugee

They took me to a place,
Where no one knew my name.
No one knew where my mama could be.
The bars were made of steel,
And my blanket was tinfoil,
And they said I'd be a deportee.

But they didn't know my home,
To send me back where I came from,
Or if I still had a family.
So I sit behind these bars, thinking.
Does mama see the same stars,
Or have they made her a deportee?

Remember what I tell you,
Or they'll treat you just the same.
If you're poor
and wanting to be free,
Don't leave your crib!
Don't leave your crib!
Don't leave your crib!
Till you know your mama's name,
Or you'll end up as a refugee.

My Most Favorite Thing in the Whole Wide World

By Elena Sichrovsky

"What does red look like," I ask
one night, my mother's
arm around me.

"Red," she begins, "feels like a
lamp you just plugged in
the socket. The glass bulb is cold
until the flicker warms the
sides, spreading from your fingertips
to your heart."

"What about blue?"

"Blue tastes like melting ice cream
dripping down a crumbling cone
on a windy autumn day.
Your lips are sticky, so you
put out your tongue to lick up
the last drop."

"And yellow?"

"Yellow sounds like an egg
cracking open on the side of the nest.
Mommy bird perches on the edge,
waiting for the chirping fluff of feathers

27

to come and take its first step
of new life."

"And me?" I ask, drawing closer
to the light of her smile
shining down on me.
"What do I look like?"

She pulls me into her arms. I hear
her breath quivering, I feel
her tears between my fingers
on her cheek. She whispers,
"You, my child, you look like
my most favorite thing in the whole wide
world."

Paper, Ink, and Time

By Mary Da Prato

I need these things to write a poem:
Paper, ink, and time
Patience, practice, solitude
And many words that rhyme

A pen and perseverance
A willingness to try
To trust I have the power
To make my words jump off the page and fly

Poetry for the Thoughtful Young

Conrad the Dachshund Steps Out

By Nancy Brewka-Clark

He walks in beauty like a knight
with muzzle held up high.
Nothing can escape this wiener's
winning bright-brown eye.
Conrad loves to go a-trotting
and a-sniffing, stubby legs
reminiscent of a pirate's,
being little more than pegs.
His deep love of admiration
always draws him to a place
where people 'ooh' and 'aah'
and compliment him to his face.
He likes a friendly pat or two
upon his velvet head, and if
you choose to scratch his back,
it's next best to being fed.
The Number One treat in his life
is ice cream in a cup, vanilla

being the favored flavor since
he was a pup. At night he sleeps
in his own bed, a pillow on the floor.
Curling up with nose to toes,
he quivers with each snore.
Each morning when he steps outside
beside his loving master,
he knows there's so much fun ahead
his tail goes fast, then faster.

Slaying Dragons (What She Thought)

By Nancy Binzen

You know,
Deep down inside
She really did think
She could
Slay her own dragons.

But of course,
She'd never say that thought
Out loud.

Slaying dragons was
A job for men,
After all,
And she liked
Being a woman.

No, far better to be
Helpless,
She decided,
To let herself
Get tied in knots
So a man could save her.

Better to slay her thoughts
Than take the risk
She might be alone
For the rest of her life.

Because once you've killed
Your first dragon,
There's no turning back.

Life is Perpetual Motion

By Steve Denehan

Life is perpetual motion,
it never knows when to stay put.
It can comfort you just like an ocean,
it can sting like a thorn in your foot.
But one thing to always remember,
if life had no sadness or pain,
you wouldn't appreciate sun in December,
or coming in out of the rain.

Poetry for the Thoughtful Young

What Would You Do with a Mini Canoe?

By Rob Carney

What would you do
with a mini canoe?
And where would you keep it
when you were through?

Would you shrink yourself down
and find a big puddle
and paddle around
way out in the middle?

Would you shrink yourself small—
the size of a bee—
and go to the tide pools
at the edge of the sea
where the starfish and crabs
will look larger than you?
What would you do with a mini canoe?

You could float in your alphabet soup,
and each letter
would be so much bigger
and taste so much better,

or float in the bathtub—
wide as the ocean—
and paddle real fast
or row in slow motion.

These are just some
of the things you can do
when you're mini enough
for a mini canoe.

But where would you keep it
when you were through
and changed back again
to your own normal size
with your regular feet, hands,
mouth, nose, and eyes?

Maybe you'd put it away in your pocket,
or into a drawer with a keyhole
and lock it,

or up by your toothbrush
next to the sink,

in the dish on the floor
where the cat gets a drink,

or under your pillow
so all night you'll dream
of the oceans you've been to,
the puddles and streams.

Mini canoes can fit anywhere.
There's plenty of room up here
or down there.
Just be sure to remember
wherever you choose...

because it's no fun to look
for lost mini canoes.

The Duties of a Cat

By Jenny Blackford

1
A cat must stand or walk on
every piece of paper.
The pawprints must be deep
and visible.
Extra points for mud,
or if the work was due the next day.

2
White cats must sleep on black clothes,
black cats must sleep on white.
Tabbies and torties are lucky;
Their shed hair shows well on any colour.
Extra points for sleeping on the crisp,
warm stack of finished ironing.

3
A cat's furry belly is irresistible.
Demand a tummy-tickle,
then claw them when they dare.
Extra points for acting hurt
when they pull their bleeding limbs away.
Demand a treat as consolation.

4
A cat must jump onto a lap and purr
only when they have something
more urgent to do than scritch your ears.

Meow more loudly when you hear
the subtle rustling of their approaching
deadlines.
Extra points for going to sleep
draped over the writing arm.

5

In fair exchange for food and constant adoration,
you must quell the enemies of the household.
Moths are insidious. They must be vanquished.
Dogs are beneath your notice, and must be
ignored.
Mice must be hunted.
For extra points, deposit the live mice under
their beds as an excellent gift.

6

Whenever possible, sleep on their chests.
They find this soothing. Extra points
for loud purring and kneading
their throats with your paws.
Extra points for leaving claws unsheathed.

7

The noblest occupation for a cat, by far,
is killing the bathmat. Every bathmat,
in every bathroom, must be quelled daily
by heavy-duty scrunching. Always
kick them with your hind legs.
This dangerous task is best undertaken at night,
when the humans won't distract you with their
terrified laughter. They will be grateful
in the morning. For extra points,
demand more treats as your reward.

The Toddler's Lament

By Emily Martha Sorensen

I do not want to take a nap,
I want to stay on Mommy's lap.

I do not want to go to bed,
I want to play with Dad instead.

I do not want to go to sleep!
Don't make me, or I'll gnash and weep.

I do not want a turned-off light,
And if you try, I'll scream and fight.

I do not want to take a nap!
I zzzzzzzzz

Poetry for the Thoughtful Young

Heavy Weather

By Bruce Boston

If gravity changed
like the weather,
covering the planet
in waves and pockets,

fronts and depressions,
there would be days
on which we could
not move an inch.

We would lie helpless,
strapped to the
slowly turning Earth
by a rain of weight

that limited both our
breath and movement.
We would have time
to consider the nature

of such an existence,
to daydream about
an end of the storm
and those perfect

feather days when we
could fly like birds
over cities and forests
as if we had wings.

Fairy Tale

By Gwyndyn Alexander

Once upon a time
there was a little girl.

She was raised to know
that she was the hero.
She was the dragon.
She was the fairy godmother.
She was the driving force
of the story.

She knew she could be anything,
do anything.

She grew up strong
and independent
and fierce.

She grew up knowing
'true love' is the result
of long, hard, mutual work,
and not a passive thing
without consent.

She grew up knowing
she could fight and defeat
the monsters.

She grew up wearing pants.
She grew up knowing
her body was her own.

She grew up knowing gender
is fluid,
and she could be whoever, whatever,
she felt was right.

She grew up knowing violence
is not affection,
that if a boy hit her,
it was wrong, and actionable,
and not a sign of love.

She grew up loving math,
and science,
and was told that she could be
an astronaut,
a construction worker,
President of the United States,
free from stigma based on sex.

She grew up knowing
love is love,
no matter who is doing the loving.

She grew up knowing
hate is not heritage,
and lies are not
alternative facts.

She grew up free
and confident.

She felt no need to diet.

She wore makeup when she pleased,
or none at all.
She wore overalls,
short skirts,
combat boots,
high heels,
and she knew that nothing she wore
was license for men
to touch her or hurt her.

She grew up free,
in a world that respected her,
and saw her as equal and valid.

She grew up to fight
for the rights of others,
for justice,
for progress.

She grew up indomitable.

And she lived
happily ever after.

Do

By McCollonough Ceili

Do fairies fly in summer skies,
On golden wings so high?

Do dragons make fire burn and gather
shiny things?

Of course, my child, in thy dreams.

Where water turns to crystal ice,
Skated on by talking mice.

Visit your dreams my child,
For there, all is wild.

Sharks and seals together play,
Within a silver bay.

The ocean tastes honey-sweet,
And milk salty as the sea.

My child, enter thy dreams,
When moonbeams beckon thee.

Inside you shall see,
All thy dreams can be.

Poetry for the Thoughtful Young

Nursery Rhyme

By Shefali Poojary

My cat Kuna won't eat fish,
So I served the fish in a pretty dish.

The fish Kuna did not touch,
But she liked the dish very much.
She ate the dish gulped-in-a-gush.

I served the fish in a nice bowl,
She ate the bowl in a slurpin-roll.

I served the fish in a fine spoon,
She ate the spoon in a lickety-roon.

Gone was all our silverware,
Our kitchen seemed 'mpty and bare.

Soon Kuna's tummy,
Felt a little crummy.

Suddenly her tummy exploded!
Dishes, bowls, and spoons unloaded.

Then her tummy felt all right,
She looked all better and bright.

She still did not touch the fish,
I didn't dare give her another dish.

The Color of My Skin

by Rucha Dixit

I may be a dancer, a painter or rabbi,
I may be a pilot spinning the sky,
I may be a swimmer or a wrestler who's just too thin,
How would you know me by the color of my skin?

I may be a diver, a racer, or tribal chief,
I may be something contrary to your belief,
I may have a brown, black, or white chin,
How would you know me by the color of my skin?

I may be a beginner or an X-factor winner,
I may be a royal or an ordinary commoner,
I may have been born in Mumbai, Kenya, or Berlin,
How would you know me by the color of my skin?

You can only know me by being a friend,
You can only know me in the time we spend,
Who knows, we may find out how much we're akin,
How would you know me by the color of my skin?

Look around and in nature you shall see,
Wherever you look there's variety.
There are flamingos, monkeys, and dolphins,
How would you know me by the color of my skin?

No two leaves on a tree are the same,
And that's what makes it fun not mundane.
Each of us is unique in our own special way,
The color of my skin doesn't matter anyway.

Poetry for the Thoughtful Young

The Kraken

By Emily Martha Sorensen

A merchant ship set sail
alone in the water.
It was caught by pirates.
There was a great slaughter.

They raided the rations.
They plundered the treasure.
"We had you for lunch!"
they cried with great pleasure.

They blasted their cannons.
The merchant ship drowned.
A terrible kraken
perked up at the sound.

Their desperate battle
was only for naught.
The great kraken crunched them.
"Yum, dinner!" it thought.

And then the great kraken,
a sailor's worst dread,
swam by a sea dragon.
"Mm, breakfast," it said.

Upstarts

By Jane Yolen

". . .the upstart strategies of a cat in boots."
—introduction, Feathers, Paws, Fins, and Claws, edited
by Schacker and Jones.

Don't all kingdoms rise and fall
on the backs of the upstarts,
the rebels, and insurrectionists
with their hurried ideas,
burning visions, unsheathed claws.

Puss' notion of raising up a master
is no worse than the machinations
of a booted Bismark or Stalin,
fingers stained with the blood
of followers who are mice to them.

Puss has given fortune to his boy,
named him Fortunato to sustain the
legend.
He settles down in much comfort,
a pillow by the fire, warm milk in a bowl,
never dreaming upstarts in turn become
the enemy.

Poetry for the Thoughtful Young

The world moves up and down
carrying its heavy burdens of blood,
mice becoming cats, cat becoming mice.
We are all mince in the mouths
of such strategists, such strategies.

God, the Girl, and the Pony

By Margaret Cook and Annette Ilowiecki

A little girl knelt by her bedside to pray,
"God, send me a pony, I want one today."
A pony can trot and gallop and play.
A pony can stomp and snort and neigh.
We'd ride through green pastures so happy and free,
In sunlight and moonlight and close to the sea.
"I'd brush it! I would! And curry its coat.
I'd feed it some hay, but only one oat."

God shook his head and furrowed his brow,
"A pony, my dear? And you want it right now?"
"A pony?" He said, "In this day and age,
What's wrong with you girl, is your head in a haze?"

"Ponies, my dear, are not all that you think,
They're wonderful creatures, but sometimes they stink!"
"Be certain you have a super large scoop.
Ponies, young lady, produce lots of poop.

"I'm strong," she replied. "I can handle the smell.
I know I can scoop poop ever so well."
"Well OK," God said, "If you still insist,
A pony for you I'll put on my list."

She ran to the barn and opened the door
To see her new pony go poop on the floor.
She scrambled astride and kicked at its side,
Hoping to get her very first ride.

It whirled and bucked her right off of its back.

"*BAD PONY!*" she shouted and gave it a whack.
With ears laid back and a frown on its face,
The pony skedaddled right out of that place.

God sighed when he heard the little girl say,
"Thank you for sending that pony away!"
God drummed his fingers in rapid succession.
"This girl," He decided, "Must learn a life lesson."
He gave a loud whistle, no note did it lack,
And the very next day, the *PONY CAME BACK!*

The Parrot

By Heather Wastie

I once drew a parrot,
but it looked like a carrot,
all orange with feathers of green.

So I then drew a carrot,
but it looked like a parrot,
the most beautiful parrot you've seen.

So I rubbed out the 'p',
and I changed it to 'c'.
and I rubbed out the 'c'
and I changed it to 'p'.

Now my carrot's a parrot,
and my parrot's a carrot,
and nobody knows except me!

Poetry for the Thoughtful Young

Diamonds and Toads: The Sequel

By Lorraine Schein

You'd think the younger daughter was
lucky—
speaking in diamonds, jewels and gold
when she talked—
but she had to be watched by the royal
guard
everywhere she sat or walked
because thieves wanted the treasures
that fell from her mouth when she
conversed,
so tried to kidnap her, and hold her
hostage
for ransom or worse.
Her husband, the prince, worried
constantly about her
and developed heart palpitations and an
anxiety disorder.

Meanwhile, the older daughter
(driven into the forest alone, because she
talked so ugly)
met a nice herpetologist who found
the many species slithering from her
mouth fascinating to study.
He also appreciated her honesty
and how her speech was never glitzy.

So, unlike her little sister, the older
daughter never had to worry
about someone not liking her for herself
and led a simpler, safer life
free from overscrutiny.

Innocent Choice: for Kate Emily Yuan

By yuan changming

Enshrined tightly
Within a car seat,
This little Buddha
Agitates furiously.

I would rather crawl
On the dirt ground,
Than be driven around
Like a caged frog!

Moon Snail Charioteer

By Meggie Nelson

Go swift into sleep, and sweet into
dreams.
Ride the silver moon snail along silver
moonbeams.
Spread trails spun from stardust across
velvet skies,
As through the distance between us I sing
lullabies.
Because no matter how far away we may
seem,
I'll keep you safe, through good or bad
dreams.
And darling, sweet love, my sweetheart
divine,
Always, always, you'll always be mine.

A Mouse in Granny's House

By Sylvia Rouss

The folks in Silly Town are helpful, indeed!
They'll come to assist whoever's in need!

"There's a mouse in my house," Granny
said with a shout.
"Who in this town will get this mouse
out?"

The baker came running, with his large
tabby cat.
"She'll catch that mouse. I'm sure about
that!"
The cat meowed,
But the mouse stayed in the house.

The butcher came running, with his sad-
looking hound.
"There's no need to worry, that mouse will
be found!"
The dog barked, and the cat meowed,
But the mouse stayed in the house.

The grocer came running, holding a goose.
"She'll snatch that mouse when I let her
loose!"
The goose honked, the dog barked, and
the cat meowed,
But the mouse stayed in the house.

The clown came running, with his pony
ready to play.
"When the mouse sees her kick, he won't
want to stay!"
The pony neighed, the goose honked, the
dog barked, and the cat meowed,
But the mouse stayed in the house.

Grandpa came running, with his big,
brown cow.
"I'm sure she'll frighten that mouse right
now!"
The cow mooed, the pony neighed, the
goose honked, the dog barked, and the cat
meowed,
But the mouse stayed in the house.

A girl came running, with her monkey,
wiry and hairy.
"I'm sure the mouse will find him quite
scary!"
The monkey screeched, the cow mooed,
the pony neighed, the goose honked, the
dog barked, and the cat meowed,
But the mouse stayed in the house.

Then a boy came running, with a small
cheese treat.
"I think that mouse might just want to
eat!"
The mouse left the house, Granny was
happy to find.
But the monkey, the cow, the pony, the
goose, the dog, and the cat all stayed
behind.

"There's a monkey, a cow, a pony, a goose,
a dog, and a cat in my house!" Granny
said with a shout.
"Who in this town will get them all out?"

Poetry for the Thoughtful Young

Peekaboo Monster

By Lorna Wood

I've turned into a monster, as anyone can
see—
Now underneath my blanket there's a
thing that isn't me.
It's scary and it's lumpy—it isn't me at
all—
But if you hug and kiss it, you can make
the blanket fall.

Then there I'll be, as good as new,
And you'll be there as well.
I know you're there when I'm away—
But me? You just can't tell.

Poetry for the Thoughtful Young

Grinner King Rictus

By Daniel Hale

When you lay down to sleep,
Alone in your bed,
The Grinner King comes for
The teeth in your head.
Rictus, his name, mouth everwide.
Upon seeing him smile, the
Queen mother died.
He comes for your teeth,
Having none of his own
To crunch up his dinner
Of stewed bits of bone.
He pulls them all bloody
And wet from your gums
With fingers so strong
They could crush you to crumbs.
He leaves not one more
Than a molar behind.
His own little joke for

Your mouth to remind.
When he's finished, his mouth
Will be straining and full,
And he'll go back, all smiles,
To the land of his rule.
He'll sing to his subjects
A groaning throat song,
His mouth far too full
To speak for too long.
His subjects will likewise
Have little to say when
Their king comes a grinning
His catch of the day.
They will watch, hardly listen,
As he gargles the sound
Of his mouth pulverizing
The teeth, grinding down.
His teeth wear out quickly
And that's why he comes
For replacements to cover
His fishy pale gums.
If you see him a-leaning
Right over your bed,
His crunch fingers pinched
For the teeth in your head,
Have a thought for his kingdom
And his choke-croaking song,
And his people who never not
Hear it for long.
Not a one of them smiles,
Not a one bears a grin.
They have nothing to make one.
Their king's already been.

Twenty-Four-Hour Taco Stand

By Evan Baughfman

John worked in the twenty-four-hour taco
stand.
It was the best one in all the land,
in the heart of the desert, amid cacti and
sand.

Business was slow,
when the early moon glowed.
Rarely did anyone show.

But one night, out of the darkness did
come
a man with skin the color of plum.
He had six heads instead of one.

"Can I have thirteen burritos,
seventeen tacos, fifty-six taquitos,
and a bag of Doritos?"

asked the strange-looking stranger.
"Don't worry, you're in no danger.
I'm a Peace-Keeping Ranger

of the Venus Patrol.
Everything's under control.
I was just on a stroll
through the Milky Way

when my stomach did say,
'I would like some Mexican food today.'"

John gave the man his order (even the
chips),
and then John said, "Thanks for making
the trip."
Next, the man slithered away,
leaving behind a very large tip

Robber Girl

By Jane Yolen

No one knows this but me.
And now you.

Once she had done her job,
rescuing Kai, that white sop of a boy,
who could not even ride a reindeer,
or tie a sled to the right bumper,
or manage an escape on his own.

Once Gerda returned him
to his own hearth, where the flames,
gave him back his own heart,
which he is now too careful about,
she left, traveling over the miles.

I know it does not say this in the story,
but Andersen was a man of cold heart,
whose loins never loosed,
who was never touched in private,
and sat at borrowed hearths.

Yes, deporable Andersen,
who understood ice,
loved the unlovables—
mainly himself, image large
in the snowy mirror of his fame.

He sent Kai home with Gerda
so she could cook his dinner,
keep his bed warm,
bundle children between them
while reading Andersen's many tales.

But no, I tell you, Gerda did not stay
longer than it took to melt the shard,
in Kai's poor, shrunken heart,
returning happily to the Robber Girl,
sharing her many wild adventures:

Bears and bearded giants;
pitted and pitiless trolls;
hairy, long-nosed Peikko and the Näkki in
her murky green:
all the usual conspirators.

Gerda and the Robber Girl,
hand in hand, arm in arm,
heart in heart, defeating the ice.
A story Andersen never dared
to tell, about Gerda or himself.

No one knows this but me.
And now you.

A Dragon at the Gate

By Gregg Chamberlain

What do you do with a dragon at your gate?
Tell him that you're sorry,
But he's just too late.
The birthday cake's been eaten
'cause all the children couldn't wait.
That's what you do with a dragon at your gate.

What do you say when a zombie's on the phone?
Tell him you're too busy
Cleaning up around your home.
Say good-bye and hang up then
Before he starts to moan.
That's what you say when a zombie's on the phone.

What should you do when a Martian visits you?
Tip your hat and shake his hand and say
"How do you do?"
Serve him tea and lemon
With a sugar lump or two.
That's what you do when a Martian visits you.

What do you do when ghosts are at your door?
One is floating above the mat.
Behind him are two more.
Tell them that you have a ghost
And you don't need any more.
That's what you do when ghosts are at your door.

Poetry for the Thoughtful Young

What should you do when a werewolf's in the room?
Eating all your chocolate
And howling at the moon?
Serve him up some castor oil
With a silver spoon.
That's what you do when a werewolf's in the room.

What should you say when a vampire calls for you?
Tell him that you're sick in bed
With an awful case of flu.
You're really very sorry,
But there's nothing you can do.
That's what you say when a vampire calls for you.

What do you do when a witch is in your bed?
With her nose so very long
And her eyes so very red?
Give her lots of medicine
For her aching head.
That's what you do when a witch is in your bed.

What do you do when monsters come to call?
Tracking slime inside your house
And cluttering up your hall?
Invite them all for shopping
Down at the local mall.
That's what you do when monsters come to call.

What do you say to the Boogeyman at night?
When you're hiding in your bed
With your new flashlight?
Ask him "Are you feeling well?
"You look an awful fright."
That's what you say to the Boogeyman at night.

Poetry for the Thoughtful Young

What do you say when a dragon's at your gate?
Tell him "I'm so sorry,
But you really have to wait.
I'm off to catch the school bus now.
Could you come back at eight?"
That's what you say when a dragon's at your gate.

Poetry for the Thoughtful Young

I Should be King

By *Elinor Clark*

All the animals gathered around,
For today was the day a new king would
be found.

But choosing a king meant they had to
agree,
And the animals all loved to argue, you
see.

"Well I should be king," cried the lion with
a roar,
"For I've been the king of the planet
before."

"No, I'd be a much better king," neighed
the horse,
"I flew into space–in a rocket, of course."

"No me," croaked the frog, "I'm a world-
famous writer."
"No me," barked the dog, "I'm an ex-ninja
fighter."

"I saved the planet from an alien attack."
"I rode 'round the world on a dinosaur's
back."

"I swam right down to the bottom of the
sea."
"I climbed to the top of the world's tallest
tree."

"I saved the jungle from a terrible fire."
 "I crossed the ocean on a thin metal wire."

"I'm older," squeaked the hare; "I'm
bolder," cried the moose;
"I'm better," growled the bear; "I'm wetter,"
honked the goose.

The animals argued and argued for days.
They squawked, and they barked, and
they hissed, and they neighed.

And each of the creatures, so sure they
were right,
Didn't notice that someone was watching
their fight.

"Listen up" came a shout; they all stopped
and looked 'round,
And saw a small snail by their feet on the
ground.

"Just look at yourselves, can't you see
what I see?
 You think *you* should be king, but I must
disagree.

"A leader is someone who listens to all,

Who helps with all problems, no matter
how small.

"What you say you've all done doesn't
matter to me.
What matters is how good a king you
would be.

"I've not saved the jungle, stopped an alien
attack,
Or flown into space in a rocket and back.

"I'm no writer or fighter, I've never been
king.
I'm not better or wetter or any such thing.

"You say you've swum deeper; you say
you've climbed higher,
But unlike all of you, at least *I'm not a
liar!*"

The animals stopped all their snarling and
growling,
Their screeching and squeaking, their
snorting and howling.

They all saw just then that their fighting
was wrong,
As the lion declared, they should all get
along.

"I suppose that we all did an unkingly
thing,
And not one of us really deserves to be
king."

"I have an idea, the greatest one ever:
Let's all share the jungle and rule it
together!"

The Collective Memories of Reptile-Kind

By M.X. Kelly

Do all the slinking, slithering snakes
sliding through the grass
dream about legs they lost
in generations past?

Does the iguana cling to its branch
and stare up at the sky,
and for just a moment close its eyes
and imagine it can fly?

If scaly reptile-kind have dreams,
then what do they inspire?
Some odd moments of déjà vu
remembering days of fire?

Poetry for the Thoughtful Young

Tale of the Town of Brigsby

By Stephanie L. Weippert

In the little town of Brigsby,
population three thousand and three.
Most people worked at the factory,
making plastic buttons and a salary

Those factory jobs kept a family well fed.

The Whyte family lorded over Brigsby town
the factory was why they had that crown.
Old Man Whyte ran the factory well,
he believed sharing the wealth made
everything swell.

But the Younger Whyte disagreed.

"Greed is good!" he'd loudly declare,
reading the news in his big armchair.
His five-year-old son often heard,
and nodded along with every word.

"Greed is Good! Greed is Good! Greed is
Good!"

At kindergarten when snack time came,
Ms. Judy, the teacher would often
exclaim,

"Timmy Whyte, you only get one."
"You need to leave enough for everyone!"

Timmy told her what Daddy had said.
"But Greed is good, Ms. Judy!"

Many years later Old Man Whyte retired,
and moved to warmer weather he desired,
leaving the factory to his son.
"Finally!" Daddy declared, "the factory is
mine to run."

And he did as he always wanted.

Timmy didn't know what Daddy did,
but he noticed that the other kids'
parents marched outside a bunch,
and everyone got free hot lunch.

Except for Timothy Whyte.

Not long after the marchers gave up,
His best friend moved away in a big
pickup.
Downtown shops all closed, even the
corner café
near the city park where Tim would play.

He missed their homemade cookies.

Next year Timmy attended boarding
school,
with a big ol' library and swimming pool,
but he missed his mom and Brigsby home.
When Tim let his thoughts wander and
roam

over happy memories long, long gone,
the best conclusion that could be drawn?

Was that his daddy had got it wrong.

Tea

By Steve Denehan

I pour the milk without stirring.
It disappears before returning,
blooming to the surface,
and reassurance blooms in me.
I learn, once again,
that some things do not change.
I am reminded
that I can be happy with small things.

Poetry for the Thoughtful Young

My Dinosaur Day

By Katey Thompson

Must I get up?
Today I know
Will be a daunting chore.
It can't be done...
Unless I go
Become a dinosaur!

So look out world,
For here I come!
I'm tough, ferocious too,
My Dino Day
Has just begun,
I'm not afraid of you.

All dinos know
They are the best,
The coolest ones around!
Let's look the part
When I get dressed...
Don't hide in the background!

Think grand! Think fun!
Today I'll wear
My tutu (it's bright pink)
And sparkly shirt
Who cares what <u>people</u> think?

As a T-Rex
I'm great, immense,
No point in playing small;
So I'll speak out,
Make no pretence
My thoughts? You'll hear them all!

"The answer's six!"
Then "Trojan Horse!"
"I didn't know that before..."
All day at school
I'm one great force
So hear my mighty roar!

Dinos are bold:
Faced with the new
They don't wail, scream or fight,
But leap right in
The unknown blue
So fine. I'll try a bite.

I've never had
Sushi 'till now
(Does it seem suspicious?)
Nigiri, rolls,
I'll try this chow
And... oooh! It's delicious!

Scared of the dark?
Yes. I don't care
For wouldn't you agree,
Dinos are brave?
Nothing out there
Is scarier than me!

With teeth and claws

Monsters beware,
You'd better hide or run!
All snug in bed
Without a care...
My Dino Day is done.

Poetry for the Thoughtful Young

Air Conditioning

By Elizabeth Glann

There was an old woman who lived in a
shoe.
It was dark, it was hot, and quite smelly,
too.
She cut out some windows 'til not much
remained.
The sandal was perfect, except when it
rained.

The Droplet

By Wenlin Tan

Once upon a time, in a tiny pond,
There was a droplet.
The droplet was clear,
Made of water from the rain.
The droplet was blue,
Like other droplets, the same.
"I'm like them too,"
Or so, she thought.
Buzzing around with other droplets.
They played, they fought,
She lived like normal droplets do.

But deep in her heart, there was a nagging
doubt,
A sapling waiting to sprout.
"Where do I come from?
Why don't I vibrate the same way other
droplets do?"
Questions for which,
Answers, she had no clue,
And so the droplet kept it a secret.

But as the droplet grew,
Of all the droplets she knew,
There was one particularly special.
Along, they swayed in the pond,

To the frequency of their special bond.
She thought things would never change,
Until one day this droplet said,
"Other droplets have all formed puddles,
And made homes around this pond, but
I can't form a puddle with you."

No longer knowing
where she belonged,
The droplet was distraught.
In the rainy thunderstorm
against the current,
She fought.
A gust of wind blew past
And lifted her
Up,
Up,
Up,
And away.
Away from the pond
She held so dear

She journeyed down the stream,
Thrown in confusion,
As if in a sweet dream,
Only to wake up
And then remember
It was a nightmare,
Not yet over.
The droplet wept, and
She became a tear.

The tear journeyed further,
Carried by the winds, she flew.
The waves engulfed her,

Welcoming her with their song
Resonance, with fervor.
It was then that she knew
It was the ocean
She had been vibrating to
All along.

She had found home,
At last.
Trust in the ocean,
Ride the wave.
Call, and
The universe will answer.

Poetry for the Thoughtful Young

Goodnight, Grandmother Moon

By Maighread MacKay

I've had my bath
My story's been read
The clock on the wall
Says it's time for bed

I've said "Goodnight, Mommy"
And "'night, Daddy," too,
But there's one more friend
I've to say goodnight to

Grandmother shines
In the black, velvet night
She brightens my room
With her silvery light

Tiny bright faeries
Slide down her soft beams
They come through my window
To enter my dreams

They laugh and they giggle
As they land on my bed
One even dances
On top of my head

"Hurray, you're here!"
I cry with glee
I'm glad they've come
To visit with me

We begin to get sleepy
Our eyes start to close
They curl up on my pillow
And one kisses my nose

"Goodnight, Grandmother Moon,"
I sigh with a yawn
As we drift off to sleep
In Dreamland 'til dawn
Grandmother smiles
With her mystical charms
And rocks us to sleep
In her comforting arms

The End?

By Nancy Binzen

"And so they lived
Happily ever after."

But then...

What do you do with yourself
When...

There are no more scaly claws
To dodge?

No more mountains of glass
To climb?

No more forests deep and dark
To enter?

When there are no more
Challenges,
What happens
Then?

Can silver goblets
And brocade dresses
Really be enough?

On second thought,
Happily ever after
Might be
Really boring.

Contributors

Bruce Boston's poems have appeared in *Asimov's SF, Analog, Weird Tales, Amazing Stories, Daily Science Fiction, Pedestal, Strange Horizons, the Nebula Awards Showcase* and *Year's Best Fantasy and Horror.* His poetry has received the Bram Stoker Award, the *Asimov's* Readers Award, and the Rhysling and Grand Master Awards of the SFPA. http://bruceboston.com/.

Delaren Siverson is a mother of three and a writer. After earning a degree from CSUN, she began writing. She lives in Simi Valley, CA with her daughter and her cat. Daniel Hale writes short stories of horror and dark fantasy. His work has been published in several anthologies and his debut collection, The Library Beneath the Streets.

Elena Sichrovsky is an Austrian citizen currently living in Shanghai, China. She grew up reading stories to her nine younger brother and sisters. She's now a student at the Shanghai University of Engineering Science and is a member of The Shanghai Writing Workshop. She also loves to write short stories and is working on finishing her first novel.

Elinor Clark is a recent Philosophy graduate hailing from Leeds in the North of England. She has work published or forthcoming in a number of publications including Strix, Book XI, Printed Words, and B Cubed B Press. Please check out more of her writing at elinorclark.yolasite.com.

Elizabeth Glann is a former teacher and librarian and is also a freelance writer. Her poems and stories have appeared in many children's magazines. She lives in Arvada, Colorado.

Emily Martha Sorensen writes clean fantasy with clever characters and lots of humor. She's been known to write about baby dragons, mischievous fairies, and heroines who can't shut their mouths. No resemblance to the author . . . honest . . . You can find out more about her at http://www.emilymarthasorensen.com.

Evan Baughfman is a middle school teacher and author. Much of his writing success has been as a playwright. He's had many different plays produced across the globe. A number of his scripts can be found at online resources,

Drama Notebook and New Play Exchange. Evan also writes horror fiction and screenplays. More information is available at his website www.evanbaughfman.com

Gregg Chamberlain is a community newspaper reporter, living in rural Ontario, Canada, with his missus, Anne, and their two cats, who let the humans think they are in charge. Gregg has been a happy reader since childhood and enjoys all sorts of nonsense poems, funny rhymes, and limericks. He is proud to be part of the B Cubed Family.

Gwyndyn T. Alexander is a New Orleans poet and artist. She alternates between creating words and creating costumes, and often confuses the two. She is the benevolent dictator of a tiny nation state consisting of one husband, one cat, and an embarrassing amount of glitter. Her work can be found at: https://www.amazon.com/Gwyndyn-T-Alexander/e/B00N7BMYGC/ref=dp_byline_cont_book_1

Heather Wastie lives in Worcestershire, England where she was Writer in Residence at the Museum of Carpet in 2013 and county Poet Laureate in 2015/16. She has published eight poetry collections. Her busy schedule of poetry commissions and performances includes oral history interpretations, tours by canal with Alarum Theatre, and a Nationwide Building Society advertisement. For more, see www.WastiesSpace.co.uk.

Isobel Horsburgh

Jane Yolen is the author of 391 published books as of the end of 2019. She has six honorary doctorates from New England colleges and universities, and a past president of SFWA, and began the New England region for SCBWI and was on SCBWI's board for 45 year. She writes a poem a day for over 1,100 subscribers.

Jenny Blackford writes poems and stories for people of all ages, usually with a tinge of myth and legend, science, or deep time. Over 30 of her short stories and over 50 of her poems have appeared in Australian and international anthologies and journals.

Jim Johnston co-writes with many musical collaborators: Úna Clarkin, Stephen Dunwoody, John Lindsay, Edelle McMahon, Ronan McSorley, Brigid O'Neill, Alan Patterson, all to be found on the usual musical distribution sites. Forthcoming – J'mok. His plays have been staged in Ireland and Belgium. His book of poetry: "Available Light": https://sites.google.com/a/lapwingpublications.com/lapwing-store/jim-johnston. He is married to Jean and has two grown-up sons.

Katey Thompson is usually found with ink stained fingers (from writing stories), or with her nose stuck in a book (from reading them), preferably with a pot of mint tea nearby. A toy maker and balloon artist, she loves sushi and wool socks. On her own dinosaur days, she prefers to be a Tyrannosaurus Rex.

Lorna Wood is a violinist and writer in Auburn, Alabama. Her poetry has appeared in Poetry South (2018 Pushcart Prize nominee), Five:2:One (#thesideshow), and Luminous Echoes (poems shortlisted for Into the Void's 2016 poetry contest), among others. She has also published fiction, creative nonfiction, and scholarly essays, and she is Senior Editor of Gemini Magazine. She blogs at lornawoodauthor.wordpress.com.

Lorraine Schein is a New York poet and writer whose work has appeared in VICE Terraform, Strange Horizons, and Wild Musette, and in the anthologies Tragedy Queens: Stories Inspired by Lana del Rey & Sylvia Plath (Clash Books), and Eighteen (Underland Press). The Futurist's Mistress, her poetry book, is available from www.mayapplepress.com.

M.X. lives in St. Petersburg, Florida with her partner, Val, a coffee pot, and their three cats. Her work has appeared in Star*Line,, Abyss & Apex, Scifaikufest, Queer Sci-Fi and other magazines and anthologies across the known 'verse. M.X.'s website can be summoned with the typed incantation of http://mxkelly.weebly.com/.

Maggie Maxwell has been writing stories that make physicists roll in their graves since 1994. She currently lives in Durham, NC with her husband, the ghosts of all the plants she's killed, and a large number of overworked and underpaid bookshelves. She can be found on Twitter as @wanderingquille.

Contributors

Maighread MacKay is the pen name of Margaret Hefferman, a Canadian author and visual artist from Durham Region in Ontario. She is a member of the Writer's Community of Durham Region (WCDR), the VFA (Visionary Fiction Allicance) and SINC (Sisters in Crime) – Toronto Chapter.

Margaret Cook and her daughter, **Annette Ilowiecki**, work together to create stories, poems, and songs that delight and inspire readers of all ages. They are both members of the Stormy Night Writer's Society in Cassopolis, MI. To learn more about them, email Ponybook123@gmail.com or visit Facebook page Don't They Just Set You To Dreaming?

Mary Da Prato is an early childhood development specialist who holds an internationally recognized AMI (Association Montessori Internationale) Primary Diploma for teaching children approximately two-and-a-half through six years of age. She has written more than twenty-five books about the Montessori Method, many of which are available in public libraries. Visit her website at http://themontessorimysteryunveiled.weebly.com.

Mccollonough Ceili discovered her love for writing when asked to record her memories of childhood adventures created on a secluded island. Since Noria's publication in 2009 Mccollonough has written several stories for readers of all ages. Her work can be found at https://www.amazon.com/author/mccollonoughceili.

Meggie Nelson received her degree in creative writing from George Mason University and is desperately trying to complete her in-progress novels. Currently, she lives in Fairfax, Virginia with her boyfriend and four ferrets (Helflyg, Rhino, Claude, and Badger). Find her on Twitter at @alicatskratches and in Forty Two Books' upcoming Strange Stories anthology. (She's also a tattoo apprentice, Instagram @needleandmink!)

Melanie Harding-Shaw is a speculative fiction writer, policy geek and mother-of-three from Wellington, New Zealand. Her short fiction has appeared in a range of publications, including another story for children in The Young Explorer's Adventure Guide Volume 6. You can find her on Twitter and Facebook, or at https://www.melaniehardingshaw.com/.

Nancy Binzen is a practicing storyteller and curator of the San Francisco Bay Area's only monthly storytelling event, Tales with Tea, exclusively featuring traditional tales (fairy, folk, myth, legend) and professional tellers. She's also a shamanic practitioner, Celtic rune reader, and local environmental and social justice activist. Her work has been published in West Marin Review and Sonder Midwest.

Nancy Brewka-Clark's poems, short stories, drama, and nonfiction have appeared in periodicals and anthologies published by Red Hen Press, University of Iowa Press, Southeast Missouri State University Press, and Routledge among others. Her debut poetry collection *Beautiful* is available through Kelsay Books and Amazon.

Paul Freeman lives and works in the Middle East. His weirdest published work is his 18,500-word Canterbury tale (in rhyming couplets and iambic pentameters) titled Robin Hood and Friar Tuck - Zombie Killers. He's the author of three published novels and numerous short stories, poems, and less-than-academic articles. He doesn't have a cat, but wishes he was one.

Rob Carney is the author of eight books, including The Book of Sharks (Black Lawrence Press, 2018, https://www.blacklawrence.com/the-book-of-sharks/), Accidental Gardens (Stormbird Press, 2020) and The Last Tiger Is Somewhere (Unsolicited Press, 2020), a collection of poems responding to the news co-written with Scott Poole. He lives in Salt Lake City.

Robert Dawson teaches mathematics at a Nova Scotian university. He has been writing science fiction and poetry for almost ten years. His other activities include fencing, hiking, and volunteering with a Scout troop. His preferred mode of transportation is a bicycle.

Rucha Dixit was born and raised in India. After 13 years in the software industry and having both her babies, she realized that she was meant to write. She channeled her passion and experience as a new mother into a self-published book, For New Mums, on Amazon. She lives with her husband and two children in London, U.K.

Contributors

Shefali Poojary is an Education Consultant who works for various non-profit organizations. She works with underserved communities in cities and remote villages across India. Shefali's poems have been published by Narrow Road magazine and The Indian Periodical. She currently lives in Chennai with her husband; her newborn; and her cat Kuna, who inspired this poem.

Sheila Kerwin is retired faculty of Early Childhood Education. Her poems have appeared in Hello, High Five, Babybug, Ladybug, and Caterpillar Magazine. Her blog, Sensiforous, focuses on young children and child development topics. When not working on poetry or picture books, she consults in Early Childhood Education, conducts workshops for teachers, writes piggyback songs, and substitute teaches in local public schools.

Stephanie Weippert Stephanie Weippert writes because of a slug. Long ago, a sci-fi convention sent out an anthology call for slug stories because of their slug mascot. This tickled Stephanie's funny bone, so she wrote her very first story. Of course, it got rejected, but the writing bug bit and she's been writing ever since. Go to patreon.com/stephanieweippert to read more.

Steve Denehan lives in Ireland with his wife Eimear and daughter Robin. He is a widely published, award-winning poet and the author of two chapbooks and two collections (one upcoming with Salmon Press). He has been nominated for The Pushcart Prize, Best of the Net, and Best New Poet.

Sylvia Rouss is the award-winning author and early childhood educator who created the popular Sammy Spider and The Littlest Books. As an early-childhood educator, the children in her classroom have been her inspiration. Sylvia has lectured throughout the United States, Europe, and Israel. Her website is www.sylviarouss.com.

Varya Kartishai is a Philadelphia writer/artist who occupies a c.1800 former farmhouse in Center City Philly with Mike Piper, her sculptor/painter husband and two large rescue cats. She feels very strongly about the refugee situation, both as a human being and as a first-generation immigrant whose family was treated with more decency when they arrived in the last century.

Wenlin Tan is a Singaporean artist and movement educator who works across words, visuals and movement to create spaces, physical or abstract, to facilitate dialogue and tell stories. Her works have been exhibited at Singapore Art Week, Book Week Scotland and Dublin art book fair. Instagram: https://www.instagram.com/wenlintellsstories/

Yuan Changming published monographs on translation before leaving China. With a Canadian PhD in English, Yuan edits Poetry Pacific with Allen Yuan in Vancouver. Credits include ten Pushcart nominations and publications in Best of the Best Canadian Poetry: Tenth Anniversary Edition, BestNewPoemsOnline and 1,709 other literary outlets across 45 countries.

Yuvia Hernández Cháirez is an ESL Spanish teacher living in Ciudad Juárez, Mexico. She is the author of The Lost (2007), De la luna y otros vicios (2007), and A Dreamer's Realm (2007). Yuvia blogs at http://pandanotebook.blogspot.com/.

Thanks to all of you.
It's been a hoot.
Bob B

www.ingramcontent.com/pod-product-compliance
Lightning Source LLC
Chambersburg PA
CBHW032137040426
42449CB00005B/283